U0111780

大展好書　好書大展

品嘗好書　冠群可期

▲作者的少林拳　Shaolin Boxing of the Author

▲武術雜誌上的耿軍
Geng Jun on the Cover of Wushu Magazine

▲英法武術代表團訪問孟州少林武術院
The Wushu Delegation of France and UK is visiting the Meng zhou Shaolin Wushu Institute

▲作者部分弟子參加武打片拍攝
Parts of students of author take part in fliming Acrobatic fighting film

▲作者與恩師素法大師
The Author and his Teacher Grandmaster Sufa

▲作者指導女兒耿瑞濤練功
The Author is coaching his daughter to practise her skill

▲作者與原國家武術協會主席張耀庭
The Author and the former Chairman of the Chinese Wushu
Association Zhang Yaoting

▲作者的少林拳　Shaolin Boxing of the Author

▲武術雜誌封面上的耿軍
Geng Jun on the Cover of Wushu Magazine

▲作者與恩師素法大師
The Author and his Teacher Grandmaster Sufa

▲ 作者率領國外弟子朝拜少林寺　Author leads foreign students to visit Shaolin Temple

▲作者與武僧教頭德揚師兄在捶譜堂
In Chuipu Hall, the author and his senior fellow apprentice
who is also the wushu monk teacher deyang

▲作者與中國政協副主席萬國權
The Author and the vice Chairman of the Chinese People's Political
Consultative Conference（CPPCC）Wan Guoquan

▲作者傳藝國際黑帶功夫總會
The Author is teaching his Wushu skill in International
Black Belt Kungfu Federation

▲作者指導兒子耿鵬飛練功
The Author is coaching his son Geng Pengfei to practise
his skill

少林傳統功夫漢英對照系列　❷

Shaolin Traditional Kungfu Series Books　❷

Seven-star Mantis Boxing（White-Ape Offering Book）

耿　軍　著

Written by Geng Jun

大展出版社有限公司

作者簡介

　　耿軍（法號釋德君），1968 年 11 月出生於河南省孟州市，係少林寺三十一世皈依弟子。中國武術七段、全國十佳武術教練員、中國少林武術研究會副秘書長、焦作市政協十屆常委、濟南軍區特警部隊特邀武功總教練、洛陽師範學院客座教授、英才教育集團董事長。1989 年創辦孟州少林武術院、2001 年創辦英才雙語學校。先後獲得河南省優秀青年新聞人物、全國優秀武術教育家等榮譽稱號。

　　1983 年拜在少林寺住持素喜法師和著名武僧素法大師門下學藝，成爲大師的關門弟子，後經素法大師引薦，又隨螳螂拳一代宗師李占元、金剛力功于憲華等大師學藝。在中國鄭州國際少林武術節、全國武林精英大賽、全國武術演武大會等比賽中 6 次獲得少林武術冠軍；在中華傳統武術精粹大賽中獲得了象徵少林武術最高榮譽的「達摩杯」一座。他主講示範的 36 集《少林傳統功夫》教學片已由人民體育音像出版社出版發行。他曾多次率團出訪海外，在國際武術界享有較高聲譽。

　　他創辦的孟州少林武術院，現已發展成爲豫北地區最大的以學習文化爲主、以武術爲辦學特色的封閉式、寄宿制學校，是中國十大武術教育基地之一。

Brief Introduction to the Author

Geng Jun（also named Shidejun in Buddhism）, born in Mengzhou City of Henan Province, November 1968, is a Bud–dhist disciple of the 31st generation, the 7th section of Chinese Wu shu, national "Shijia" Wu shu coach, Vice Secretary General of China Shaolin Wu shu Research Society, standing committee member of 10th Political Consultative Conference of Jiaozuo City, invited General Kungfu Coach of special police of Jinan Military District, visiting professor of Luoyang Normal University, and Board Chairman of Yingcai Education Group. In 1989, he estab–lished Mengzhou Shaolin Wu shu Institute; in 2001, he estab –lished Yingcai Bilingual School · He has been successively awarded honorable titles of "Excellent Youth News Celebrity of Henan Province" "State Excellent Wu shu Educationalist" etc.

In 1983, he learned Wu shu from Suxi Rabbi, the Abbot of Shaolin Temple, and Grandmaster Sufa, a famous Wu shu monk, and became the last disciple of the

Grandmaster. Then recom–mended by Grandmaster Sufa, he learned Wu shu from masters such as Li Zhanyuan, great master of mantis boxing, and Yu Xianhua who specializes in Jingangli gong. He won the Shaolin Wu shu champion for 6 times in China Zhengzhou International Wu shu Festival, National Competition of Wu lin Elites, National Wu shu Performance Conference, etc. and one "Damo Trophy" that symbolizes the highest honor of Shaolin Wu shu in Chinese Traditional Wu shu Succinct Competition. 36 volumes teaching VCD of Shaolin Traditional Wu shu has been published and is –sued by People´s Sports Audio Visual Publishing House. He has led delegations to visit overseas for many times, enjoying high reputation in the martial art circle of the world.

Mengzhou Shaolin Wu shu Institute, established by him, has developed into the largest enclosed type boarding school of Yubei (north of Henan Province) area, which takes knowledge as primary and Wu shu as distinctiveness, also one of China´s top ten Wu shu education bases.

序　言

中華武術源遠流長，門類繁多。

少林武術源自嵩山少林寺，因寺齊名，是我國拳系中著名的流派之一。少林寺自北魏太和十九年建寺以來，已有一千五百多年的歷史。而少林武術也決不是哪一人哪一僧所獨創，它是歷代僧俗歷經漫長的生活歷程，根據生活所需逐步豐富完善而成。

據少林寺志記載許多少林僧人在出家之前就精通武術或慕少林之名而來或迫於生計或看破紅塵等諸多原因削髮爲僧投奔少林，少林寺歷來倡武，並經常派武僧下山，雲遊四方尋師學藝。還請武林高手到寺，如宋朝的福居禪師曾邀集十八家武林名家到寺切磋技藝，推動了少林武術的發展，使少林武術得諸家之長。

本書作者自幼習武，師承素喜、素法和螳螂拳李占元等多位名家，當年如饑似渴在少林寺研習功夫，曾多次在國內外大賽中獲獎。創辦的孟州少林武術院亦是全國著名的武術院校之一，他示範主講的 36 集《少林傳統功夫》教學 VCD 已由人民體育音像出版社發行。

本套叢書的三十多個少林傳統套路和實戰技法是少

林武術的主要內容，部分還是作者獨到心得，很值得一讀，該書還採用漢英文對照，使外國愛好者無語言障礙，爲少林武術走向世界做出了自己的貢獻，亦是可喜可賀之事。

張耀庭題
甲申秋月

Preface

序
言

Chinese Wushu is originated from ancient time and has a long history, it has various styles.

Shaolin Wushu named from the Shaolin Temple of Songshan Mountain, it is one of the famous styles in the Chinese boxing genre. Shaolin temple has more than 1500 years of history since its establishment in the 19th year of North Wei Taihe Dynasty. No one genre of Shaolin Wushu is created solely by any person or monk, but completed gradually by Buddhist monks and common people from generation to generation through long-lasting living course according to the requirements of life. As recording of Record of Shaolin Temple, many Shaolin Buddhist monks had already got a mastery of Wushu before they became a Buddhist monk, they came to Shaolin for tonsure to be a Buddhist monk due to many reasons such as admiring for the name of Shaolin, or by force of life or seeing through thevanity of life. The Shaolin Temple always promotes Wushu and frequently appoints Wushu Buddhist monks to go down the mountain to roam around for searching masters and learning Wushu from them. It also invites

Wushu experts to come to the temple, such as Buddhist monk Fuju of Song Dynasty, it once invited Wushu famous exports of 18 schools to come to the temple to make skill interchange, which promoted the development of Shaolin Wushu and made it absorb advantages of all other schools.

The author learned from many famous exports such as Suxi, Sufa and Li Zhanyuan of Mantis Boxing, he studied Chinese boxing eagerly in Shaolin Temple, and got lots of awards both at home and abroad, he also set up the Mengzhou Shaolin Wushu Institute, which is one of the most famous Wushu institutes around China. He makes demonstration and teaching in the 36 volumes teaching VCD of Shaolin Traditional Wushu, which have been published by Peoples sports Audio Visual publishing house.

There are more than 30 traditional Shaolin routines and practical techniques in this series of books, which are the main content of Shaolin Wushu, and part of which is the original things learned by the author, it is worthy of reading. The series books adopt Chinese and English versions, make foreign fans have no language barrier, and make contribution to Shaolin Wushu going to the world, which is delighting and congratulating thing.

Titled by Zhang Yaoting

目　錄
Contents

說　明

　　（一）為了表述清楚，以圖像和文字對動作作了分解說明，練習時應力求連貫銜接。

　　（二）在文字說明中，除特別說明外，不論先寫或後寫身體的某一部分，各運動部位都要求協調活動、連貫銜接，切勿先後割裂。

　　（三）動作方向轉變以人體為準，標明前後左右。

　　（四）圖上的線條是表明這一動作到下一動作經過的線路及部位。左手、左腳及左轉均為虛線（┈┈►）；右手、右腳及右轉均為實線（──►）。

Instructions

(i) In order to explain clearly figures and words are used to describe the actions in multi steps. Try to keep coherent when exercising.

(ii) In the word instruction, unless special instruction, each action part of the body shall act harmoniously and join coherently no matter it is written first or last, please do not separate the actions.

(iii) The action direction shall be turned taking body as standard, which is marked with front, back, left or right.

(iv) The line in the figure shows the route and position from this action to the next action. The left hand, left foot and turn left are all showed in broken line (------►) ; the right hand, right foot and turn right are all showed in real line (——►) .

基本步型與基本手型
Basic stances and Basic hand forms

圖 1

圖 2

圖 3

圖 4

圖 5

圖 6

七星螳螂拳白猿孝母

圖 7

圖 8

圖 9

圖 10

圖 11

圖 12

基本步型與基本手型

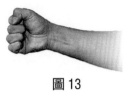

圖 13

圖 14

圖 15

圖 16

圖 17

圖 18

圖 19

圖 20

圖 21

基本步型

少林武術中常見的步型有：弓步、馬步、仆步、虛步、歇步、坐盤步、丁步、併步、七星步、跪步、高虛步、翹腳步 12 種。

弓步：俗稱弓箭步。兩腿前後站立，兩腳相距本人腳長的 4～5 倍；前腿屈至大腿接近水平，腳尖微內扣不超過 5°；後腿伸膝挺直，腳掌內扣 45°。（圖 1）

馬步：俗稱騎馬步。兩腳開立，相距本人腳長的 3～3.5 倍，兩腳尖朝前；屈膝下蹲大腿接近水平，膝蓋與兩腳尖上下成一條線。（圖 2）

仆步：俗稱單叉，一腿屈膝全蹲，大腿貼緊小腿，膝微外展，另一腿直伸平仆接近地面，腳掌扣緊與小腿成 90°夾角。（圖 3）

虛步：又稱寒雞步。兩腳前後站立，前後相距本人腳長的 2 倍；重心移至後腿，後腿屈膝下蹲至大腿接近水平，腳掌外擺 45°；前腿腳尖點地，兩膝相距 10 公分。（圖 4）

歇步：兩腿左右交叉，靠近全蹲；前腳全腳掌著地，腳尖外展，後腳腳前掌著地，臀部微坐於後腿小腿上。（圖 5）

坐盤步：在歇步的形狀下，坐於地上，後腿的大小腿外側和腳背均著地。（圖 6）

　　丁步：兩腿併立，屈膝下蹲，大腿接近水平，一腳尖點地靠近另一腳內側腳窩處。（圖7）

　　併步：兩腿併立，屈膝下蹲，大腿接近水平。（圖8）

　　七星步：七星步是少林七星拳和大洪拳中獨有的步型。一腳內側腳窩內扣於另一腳腳尖，兩腿屈膝下蹲，接近水平。（圖9）

　　跪步：又稱小蹬山步。兩腳前後站立，相距本人腳長的2.5倍，前腿屈膝下蹲，後腿下跪，接近地面，後腳腳跟離地。（圖10）

　　高虛步：又稱高點步。兩腳前後站立，重心後移，後腿腳尖外擺45°，前腿腳尖點地，兩腳尖相距一腳距離。（圖11）

　　翹腳步：在七星螳螂拳中又稱七星步，兩腿前後站立，相距本人腳長的1.5倍，後腳尖外擺45°，屈膝下蹲，前腿直伸，腳跟著地，腳尖微內扣。（圖12）

基本手型

　　少林武術中常見的手型有拳、掌、鉤3種。

　　拳：

　　分為平拳和透心拳。

　　平拳：平拳是武術中較普遍的一種拳型，又稱方拳。四指屈向手心握緊，拇指橫屈扣緊食指。（圖

13）

透心拳：此拳主要用於打擊心窩處，故名。四指併攏捲握，中指突出拳面，拇指扣緊抵壓中指梢節處。（圖14）

掌：

分為柳葉掌、八字掌、虎爪掌、鷹爪掌、鉗指掌。

柳葉掌：四指併立，拇指內扣。（圖15）

八字掌：四指併立，拇指張開。（圖16）

虎爪掌：五指分開，彎曲如鉤，形同虎爪。（圖17）

鷹爪掌：又稱鎖喉手，拇指內扣，小指和無名指彎曲扣於掌心處，食指和中指分開內扣。（圖18）

鉗指掌：五指分開，掌心內含。（圖19）

鉤：

分為鉤手和螳螂鉤。

鉤手：屈腕，五指自然內合，指尖相攏。此鉤使用較廣，武術中提到的鉤均為此鉤。（圖20）

螳螂鉤：又稱螳螂爪，屈腕成腕部上凸，無名指、小指屈指內握，食指、中指內扣，拇指梢端按貼於食指中節。（圖21）

Basic stances

Usual stances in Shaolin Wushu are: bow stance, horse stance, crouch stance, empty stance, rest stance, cross – legged sitting, T – stance, feet – together stance, seven – star stance, kneel stance, high empty stance, and toes – raising stance, these twelve kinds.

Bow stance: commonly named bow – and – arrow stance. Two feet stand in tandem, the distance between two feet is about four or five times of length of one´s foot; the front leg bends to the extent of the thigh nearly horizontal with toes slightly turned inward by less than 5°; the back leg stretches straight with the sole turned inward by 45°. (Figure 1)

Horse stance: commonly named riding step. two feet stand apart, the distance between two feet is 3~3.5 times of length of one´s foot, with tiptoes turned forward; bend knees to squat downward, with thighs nearly horizontal, knees and two tiptoes in line. (Figure 2)

Crouch stance: commonly named single split. Bend the knee of one leg and squat entirely with thigh very close to lower leg and knee outspread slightly; straighten the other leg and crouch horizontally close to floor, keep the sole turned inward and forming an included angle of 90° with lower leg. (Figure 3)

Empty stance: also named cold – chicken stance. Two feet stand in tandem, the distance between two feet is 2 times of

length of one´s foot; transfer the barycenter to back leg, bend the knee of the back leg and squat downward to the extent of the thigh nearly horizontal, with the sole turned outward by 45°; keep the tiptoe of front leg on the ground, with distance between two knees of 10cm. (Figure 4)

Rest stance: cross the two legs at left and right, keep them close and entirely squat; keep the whole sole of the front foot on the ground with tiptoes turned outward, the front sole of the back foot on the ground, and buttocks slightly seated on the lower leg of the back leg. (Figure 5)

Cross – legged sitting: in the posture of rest stance, sit on the ground, with the outer sides of the thigh and lower leg of the back leg and instep on the ground. (Figure 6)

T – stance: two legs stand with feet together, bend knees and squat to the extent of the thighs nearly horizontal, with one tiptoe on the ground and close to inner side of the fossa of the other foot. (Figure 7)

Feet – together stance: two legs stand with feet together, bend knees and squat to the extent of the thigh nearly horizontal. (Figure 8)

Seven – star stance: Seven – star step is a unique step form in Shaolin Seven – star Boxing and Major Flood Boxing. Keep the inner side of the fossa of one foot turned inward onto tiptoe of the other foot, bend two knees and squat nearly horizontal. (Figure 9)

Kneel stance: also named small mountaineering stance. Two feet stand in tandem, the distance between two feet is 2.5

times of length of one´s foot, bend knee of the front leg and squat, kneel the back leg close to the floor, with the heel of back foot off the floor. (Figure 10)

High empty stance: also named high point stance. Two feet stand in tandem. Transfer the barycenter backward, turn the tiptoe of the back leg outward by 45°, with tiptoe of front leg on the ground, and the distance between two tiptoes is length of one foot. (Figure 11)

Toes –raising stance: also named seven –star stance in Seven–star Mantis Boxing. Two legs stand in tandem, and the distance between two legs is 1.5 times of length of one´s foot. Keep the tiptoe of back leg turned outward by 45°, bend knees and squat, straighten the front leg with heel on the ground and tiptoe turned inward slightly. (Figure 12)

Basic hand forms

Usual hand forms in Shaolin Wushu are: fist, palm and hook, these three kinds.

Fist: classified into straight fist and heart–penetrating fist.

Flat fist: a rather common fist form in Wushu, also named square fist. Hold the four fingers tightly toward the palm, and horizontally bend the thumb to button up the fore finger. (Figure 13)

Heart –penetrating fist: mainly used for striking the heart part. Put four fingers together and coil –hold them, the middle finger thrusts out the striking surface of the fist, the thumb

七星螳螂拳白猿孝母

buttons up and presses the end and joint of the middle finger. （Figure 14）

Palm: classified into willow leaf palm, splay palm, tiger´s claw palm, eagle´s claw palm, fingers clamping palm.

Willow leaf palm: palm with four fingers up and thumb turned inward. （Figure 15）

Eight－shape palm: palm with four fingers up and thumb splay. （Figure 16）

Tiger´s claw palm: palm with five fingers apart, bent as hook and like tiger´s claw. （Figure 17）

Eagle´s claw palm: also named throat locking hand, with the thumb turned inward, the little finger and middle finger turned onto palm, fore finger and middle finger apart and turned inward. （Figure 18）

Fingers clamp palm: palm with five fingers apart and palm drawn in. （Figure 19）

Hook: classified into hook hand and mantis hook.

Hook hand: bend the wrist, five fingers drawn in naturally with fingertips together. This hook is used in wide range, the hook mentioned in Wushu refers to this. （Figure 20）

Mantis hook: also named mantis´ claw, bend wrist into wrist bulge upward, the ring finger and little finger bend to hold inward, with fore finger and fore middle finger turned inward and end of thumb pressed on the middle joint of the fore finger. （Figure 21）

白猿孝母套路簡介
Brief Introduction Routine to the White Ape Giving Presents to the Mother

七星螳螂拳是清初拳師王郎在研究螳螂捕蟬時運用兩臂劈、砍、刁、閃的捕鬥技巧而創編的一種象形拳法。後王郎入少林寺3年，向寺僧傳授螳螂拳法，白猿孝母是七星螳螂拳其中的一個套路，該套路剛柔並濟、長短互用、手到腳到、貫穿緊湊、節奏明快、勁整力圓、周身相合、勾摟纏封、變化無窮。

Seven－star mantis boxing is a kind of shape－simulating boxing, which was developed and compiled by Wang Lang, a boxer at early Qing Dynasty, applying the capturing and fighting skills of the two arms when he researched the scene of mantis capturing cicada. Later, Wang Lang stayed at Shao Temple for 3 years, and taught mantis boxing to the monks of this temple. White Ape Giving Presents to the Mother is one of the routines in seven－star mantis boxing, which uses the temper force with grace, both long and short actions, harmonious and consistent actions of the hands and feet, forthright rhythm, integral strength and complete force, the actions of hook, grad, twining and closing, being coherent, compact and most changeful.

白猿孝母套路動作名稱

Action Names of Routine White Ape Giving Presents to the Mother

七星螳螂拳白猿孝母

第一段　Section One

1. 預備勢
   Preparatory Posture
2. 螳螂雙封手
   Mantis close up two hands
3. 白猿出洞
   White ape comes out of the cave
4. 鎖口捶
   Mouth－locking hammer
5. 黑虎掏心捶
   Black tiger draws out heart
6. 左封右崩捶
   Left wrap and right snap hammer
7. 底漏圈捶
   Circule hammer from leaky base
8. 採三手玉環步
   Grab hands three times in jade－ring step

9. 左封右崩捶

Left wrap and right snap hammer

10. 蹬撲雙叫

Kick and pounce with double-call

第二段　Section Two

11. 轉身右圈捶

Turn body and circle right hammer

12. 裏摟採三手

Brush inward and grab hand three times

13. 撩陰捶

crotch-uppercutting hammer

14. 左封右崩捶

Left wrap and right snap hammer

15. 採三手玉環步

Grab hand three times in jade-ring step

16. 左封右崩捶

Left wrap and right snap hammer

第三段　Section Three

17. 轉身掄劈圈捶

Turn body, swing, hack and circle hammer

18. 上步掄劈圈捶

Step forward, swing hack and circle hammer

19. 邦　肘

Help elbow

20. 左封右崩捶

Left wrap and right snap hammer

21. 採三手玉環步

Grab hand three times in jade-ring step

第四段　Section Four

22. 鎖口捶

Mouth-locking hammer

23. 上步劈崩

Step forward to hack and snap

24. 螳螂千眼

Mantis with thousand eyes

25. 蓋陽掌玉環步

Cover with Yang-palm in jade-ring step

26. 戳捶

Thrust hammer

27. 轉身雙封手

Turn body and close up two hands

28. 收　勢

Closing form

白猿孝母套路動作圖解

Action Illustrtion of Routine White Ape
Giving Presents to the Mother

圖1

第一段　Section One

1.預備勢　Preparatory Posture

(1)兩腳併立；兩手自然下垂，五指併攏，貼於體
側；目視前方。（圖1）

(1) Stand upright with feet together. the hands hung
naturally with the fingers together and close to both sides of the
body. Eyes look forward.〔Figure 1〕

七星螳螂拳白猿孝母

圖 2

(2)兩手變拳上提，抱於兩腰間，拳心向上；目視左方。（圖 2）

要點：挺胸塌腰，頭正頸直；挺胸收腹，抱拳迅速。

(2) The two hands change into fists and rise, hold on the waist with the fist-palm up. Eyes look leftward.〔Figure 2〕

Key points：keep the chest out and abdomen in, the head being correctitude and neck straight. Lift the chest, draw in the abdomen and hold fists quickly．

白
猿
孝
母
套
路
動
作
圖
解

圖 3

2. 螳螂雙封手　Mantis close up two hands

（1）接上勢。身體左轉 90°，右腳提起向後撤一步；同時，右拳變掌，掌心向下，從後向身前畫掌；左拳變掌向下插掌，掌心向下，以右前臂相交於腹前；目視兩掌。（圖 3）

(1) Follow the above posture, turn the body 90° to the left, lift the right foot and take a step backward. At the same time, change the right fist into palm, swing the right palm backward to the front of the body with the palm downward, change the left fist into palm and insert the palm downward with the palm down, crossing with the right forearm in front of the abdomen. Eyes look at the two palms.〔Figure 3〕

圖 4

(2)上動不停。身體略向後傾斜；同時，兩臂屈肘，兩掌在胸前翻轉絞手，右掌心向上，掌指向右，高與頜平；左掌心向右，掌指向後，略高於右手；目視前方。（圖 4）

(2) Keep the above action, slant the body backward slightly. At the same time, bend the two elbows, turn over the two palms in front of the chest and twist the hands. Keep the right palm up with the fingers rightward, at chin height, keep the left palm rightward with the fingers backward, slightly higher than the right hand. Eyes look forward. (Figure 4)

圖 5

　　(3)上動不停。重心略前移；同時，右掌前探，虎口向上，掌心向前，高與肩平；左掌護於右肩前，掌心向右，掌指向後；目視右掌。（圖5）

　　(3) Keep the above action, slightly shift the barycenter forward. At the same time, stretch the right palm forward, keep the tiger´s mouth up, the palm forward, at shoulder height; the left palm guards in front of the right shoulder with the palm rightward and the fingers backward. Eyes look at the right palm. （Figure 5）

圖6

(4)上動不停。右臂屈肘，右掌變為螳螂鉤，吊腕回拉於胸前，鉤尖向下；同時，左掌前伸成掌指向前，掌心向下，高與肩平；目視左掌。（圖6）

(4) Keep the above action, bend the right elbow, change the right palm into mantis hook, hang the wrist and draw back to the front of the chest with the hook –tip downward. At the same time, stretch the left palm forward, keep the fingers forward and the palm down, at shoulder height. Eyes look at the left palm. (Figure 6)

白
猿
孝
母
套
路
動
作
圖
解

圖 7

(5)上動不停。左腳向後退半步，重心後移成左虛步；同時，左臂屈肘，左掌變為螳螂鈎，吊腕回拉於左膝上方，鈎尖向前，高與肩平；目視前方。（圖 7）

要點：整個動作要連貫一致，快捷有力。

(5) Keep the above action, the left foot takes half a step backward, shift the barycenter backward into left empty stance. At the same time, bend the left elbow, change the left palm into mantis hook, hang the wrist and draw it back upon the left knee with the hook –tip forward, at shoulder height. Eyes look forward.（Figure 7）

Key points: the whole action shall be coherent and consistent, rapid and forceful.

七星螳螂拳白猿孝母

圖8

3. 白猿出洞　White ape comes out of the cave

（1）接上勢。身體起立，重心前移，右腿提膝，左腿獨立；同時，左鉤手變掌向前探出，掌心斜向上，掌指向前，高與肩平；右鉤手變拳，置於右耳側，拳心向外，拳眼向下；目視前方。（圖8）

（1）Follow the above posture, lift the body, move the barycenter forward, lift the right knee with the left leg standing alone. At the same time, change the left hook hand into palm and stretch it forward, keep the palm up aslant and the fingers forward, at shoulder height; change the left hook hand into fist and place it at the side of the right ear with the fist –plane outward and the fist –hole down. Eyes look forward. （Figure 8）

白猿孝母套路動作圖解

圖 9

(2)上動不停。右腳向前跨一步，左腳隨即跟步，身微左轉，下蹲成蹬山步；同時，掄右臂向前斜劈拳，拳心向左，拳輪向下，高與肩平；左掌向裏迎擊右前臂，掌心貼於右前臂內側，掌指向上；目視前方。（圖 9）

(2) Keep the above action, the right foot takes a step forward, then the left one follows up, the body twists leftward, squats into mountaineering step. At the same time, swing the right arm and hack the fist incined forward, keep the fist – palm leftward and the palm wheel down, at shoulder height; the left palm counterpunches the right forearm inward, keep the palm close to the inner side of the right forearm with the fingers up. Eyes look forward.（Figure 9）

七星螳螂拳白猿孝母

圖 10

4. 鎖口捶　Mouth-locking hammer

接上勢。身體提起，右腳向前上一步，左腳隨即跟步成蹬山步；同時，右拳收回胸前並向右格肘，右拳置於右耳側，拳心向後，拳眼向外；左掌變拳收回腰間，隨即向前平沖，拳心向下；目視左拳。（圖 10）

白
猿
孝
母
套
路
動
作
圖
解

Follow the above posture, the body lifts, the right foot takes a step forward, then the left foot follows up into mountaineering stance. At the same time, draw back the right fist to the front of the chest and parry the elbow rightward, place the right fist at the side of the right ear with the fist–palm backward and the fist–hole outward; change the left palm into fist and draw it back on the waist, then horizontally punch the left fist forward, keep the fist–plane down. Eyes look at the left fist. (Figure 10)

圖 11

5. 黑虎掏心捶   Black tiger draws out heart

接上勢。右腳向前上步，左腳隨即跟步，身體左轉 90°，向下蹲身成馬步；同時，右拳收於腰間，隨即向右下方沖拳，拳心向下，拳眼向前，高與腰齊；左拳變掌迎擊右拳面，回收於右胸前，掌心向右，掌指向裏；目視右拳。（圖 11）

Follow the above posture, the right foot steps forward, then the left one follows up, the body turns 90° to the left and squats into horse stance. At the same time, draw the right fist on the waist, then punch the fist right downward, keep the fist–palm down and the fist–hole forward, at waist level; change the left fist into palm to counterpunch the right fist–plane, draw it back to the front of the right chest with the palm rightward and the fingers inward. Eyes look at the right fist.（Figure 11）

白猿孝母套路動作圖解

圖 12

6. 左封右崩捶
Left wrap and right snap hammer

(1)接上勢。身體右轉 90°，右腳向前上步，隨即左腳跟步，重心前移成蹬山步；同時，左手在胸前封抓變拳，拳心向下，高與肩平；右拳收抱於腰間，拳心向上；目視前方。（圖 12）

(1) Follow the above posture, the body turns 90° to the right, the right foot steps forward, then the left one follows up, shift the barycenter forward into mountaineering stance. At the same time, grab the left hand in front of the chest and change it into fist with the fist–palm down, at shoulder height; draw the right fist back and hold on the waist with the fist–palm up. Eyes look forward. (Figure 12)

圖 13

（2）上動不停。左拳屈臂回收於右胸前，拳心向下，拳面向右；右拳經左前臂內側向前崩拳，拳心向裏，拳面向上，高與頷平；目視右拳。（圖 13）

要點：崩拳要有彈性，抖肩發力，力達拳背。

（2）Keep the above action, bend the left arm and draw back the left fist to the front of the right chest with the fist–palm down and the fist–plane right ward; swing and snap the right fist forward from the inner side of the left forearm, keep the fist–palm inward and the fist–plane up, at chin height. Eyes look at the right fist.（Figure 13）

Key points: Snapping the fist shall be flexible, send the shoulders to apply force that shall reach the fist–back.

圖 14

7. 底漏圈捶　Circular hammer from leaky base

(1) 接上勢。身體起立，微向右轉，左腳向左跨一步，重心落於兩腿間；同時，右拳收抱於腰間，拳心向上；左拳變掌，從右肘下向前推出，掌心向前，掌指向上，高與肩平。（圖 14）

(1) Follow the above posture, the body stands up and turns to the right slightly, the left foot takes a step leftward, the barycenter puts in the middle of the two legs. At the same time, draw the right fist back and hold it on the waist with the fist - palm up; change the left fist into palm and push it forward from lower port the right elbow, keep the palm forward and the fingers up, at shoulder height. (Figure 14)

七星螳螂拳白猿孝母

圖 15

　　(2)上動不停。身體微向左轉，左腳收回，腳尖點地，左腿屈膝下蹲成右虛步；同時，右拳經胸前自右向左圈擊，拳心向前，拳面向左；左掌向裏迎擊右前臂內側，掌心貼於右肘內側，掌指向上；目視右前方。（圖 15）

　　(2) Keep the above action, turn the body to the left slightly, draw the left foot back with toes on ground, bend the left knee and squat into right empty stance. At the same time, the right fist circle–punch right to left through the front of the chest with the fist–palm forward and the fist–plane leftward; the left palm counterpunches the inner side of the right forearm inward, keep the palm close to the inner side of the right elbow with the fingers up. Eyes look right forward.（Figure 15）

圖 16

8. 採三手玉環步

Grab hands three times in jade-ring step

(1)接上勢。身體起立，重心前移至右腿；同時，右手向外翻腕採抓變拳，拳心斜向下，拳面向前，高與肩平。（圖 16）

(1) Follow the above posture, the body rises, move the barycenter forward to the right leg. At the same time, turn the right wrist outward and grab into fist, keep the fist – palm down and the fist – plane forward, at shoulder height.（Figure 16）

圖 17

（2）上動不停。身體略微右轉成右弓步；同時，右拳收抱於腰間，拳心向上；左拳變掌，從胸前向前封抓變拳，拳心向下，拳面向右，高與肩平；目視左拳。（圖17）

(2) Keep the above action, slightly turn the body to the right into right bow stance. At the same time, draw back the right fist and hold it on the waist with the fist－palm up; change the left fist into palm, grab it forward through the front of the chest and change it into fist, keep the fist－palm down and the fist－plane rightward, at shoulder height. Eyes look at the left fist.（Figure 17）

圖 18

　⑶上動不停。身體略向左轉；同時，右拳經左前
臂內側向前上方沖出，拳心斜向上，高與鼻齊；左拳
回收於右胸前，拳心向下；目視右拳。（圖 18）

⑶ Keep the above action, turn the body to the left slightly.
At the same time, punch the right fist upward ahead through the
inner side of the left forearm with the fist–palm up aslant, at
nose height; draw back the left fist to the front of the right chest
with the fist–palm down. Eyes look at the right fist.〔Figure
18〕

圖 19

(4)上動不停。身體向右轉 90°，右拳收回抱於腰
間，拳心向上；左拳變掌，經右臂外側向前穿掌，掌心
斜向上，掌指向左前方；目視左掌。（圖 19）

(4) Keep the above action. wist the body 90° to the right,
draw back the right fist and hold on the waist with the fist–palm
up, change the left fist into palm and thread out the palm forward
through the outer side of the right arm, keep the palm upward
aslant ad the fingers left forward. Eyes look at the left palm.
（Figure 19）

圖 20

（5）上動不停。左腳向前跨一步，隨即右腳跟步，身體向左轉 90°，蹲身成玉環步；同時，左掌翻腕變拳，向左側拉帶，拳心向左，拳眼向下，高與肩平；右拳變掌，經胸前向左下方推掌，置於左膝外側，掌心向左，掌指向前；目視左前方。（圖 20）

（5）Keep the above action. the left foot takes a step forward, then the right one follows up, the body twists and turns 90° to the left , squats into jade–ring step. At the same time, the left palm turns the wrist into fist and draws leftward, keep the fist –palm left ward and the fist–hole down, at shoulder height; change the right fist in to palm and horizontally push it left downward through the front of the chest, place it at the outer side of the left knee, keep the palm leftward and the fingers forward. Eyes look left forward.（Figure 20）

圖 21

9. 左封右崩捶
Left wrap and right snap hammer

（1）接上勢。右腳向前上步，左腳隨即跟步，向下蹲身成蹬山步；同時，右掌變拳收於右胸前，拳心向裏；左手向裏封抓變拳，拳心向下，拳眼向裏，高與肩平；目視前方。（圖 21）

(1) Follow the above posture. the right foot steps forward, then the left foot follows up, squat into mountaineering step. At the same time, change the right palm into fist and draw it back to the front of the right chest with the fist-palm inward; grab the left hand inward into fist, keep the fist-Palm down and the fist-hole inward, at shoulder height. Eyes look forward. 〔Figure 21〕

白猿孝母套路動作圖解

圖 22

(2)上動不停。左拳回收於右胸前，拳心向下，拳面向右；右拳經左前臂內側向前崩拳，拳心向裏，拳面向上，高與頜平；目視右拳。（圖 22）

要點：崩拳要有彈性，抖肩發力，力達拳背。

(2) Keep the above action. draw back the left fist to the front of the right chest, keep the fist–palm down and the fist–plane rightward; swing and snap the right fist forward through the inner side of the left forearm, keep the fist–palm inward and the fist–plane up, at chin height. Eyes look at the right fist. (Figure 22)

Key points: snapping the fist shall be flexible, send the shoulder to apply strength that shall reach the fist–back.

圖 23

10. 蹬撲雙叫
Kick and pounce with double-call

（1）接上勢。身體起立，左轉 90°，右腳向左腳後倒插步，左膝微屈，右腳跟抬起；同時，兩拳變掌，經胸前擺至身體左側，左掌心朝上，右掌心朝下，兩掌指均向左，高與腰齊；目視左掌。（圖 23、圖 23 附圖）

白
猿
孝
母
套
路
動
作
圖
解

圖 23 附圖

(1) Follow the above posture. the body stands up and turns 90° to the left, the right foot does back cross step leftward, slightly bend the left knee, and lift up the right heel. At the same time, change the two fists into palms and swing them to the left side of the body through the front of the chest. Keep the left palm up and the right one down, both the fingers of the two palms leftward, at waist height. Eyes look at the left palm. (Figure 23 Attached figure 23)

圖 24

　　(2)上動不停。重心左移，右腳踏實，左腳向左橫跨一步成右弓步；同時，兩掌抓握變拳，經胸前向右拉帶，置於右膝外側，左拳心向上，右拳心向下；目視左後方。（圖24、圖24附圖）

圖 24 附圖

(2) Keep the above action, shift the barycenter leftward, the right foot stamps firmly, the left one strides a step leftward into right bow stance. At the same time, clench the two palms and change them into fists, draw them rightward through the front of the chest and place them at the outer side of the right knee, with the left fist –palm up and the right one down. Eyes look left backward.（Figure 24、 Attached figure 24）

圖 25

第二段 Section Two

11. 轉身右圈捶
Turn body and circle right hammer

　　接上勢。身體起立，左轉 90°，右腳略向前墊步；
右拳從右向左圈擊，拳心向下，拳眼向裏，高與肩
平；左拳經腹前向左畫弧，隨即變掌向裏迎擊右前臂
內側；目視前方。（圖 25）

白
猿
孝
母
套
路
動
作
圖
解

Follow the above posture. the body stands up and turns 90° to the left, the right foot slightly skips step forward, the right fist makes circle punch rightward to leftward, keep the fist – palm down and the fist – hole inward, at shoulder height; swing the left fist leftward through the front of the abdomen to draw a curve, then change it into palm and counterpunch the inner side of the right forearm. Eyes look forward. 〔Figure 25〕

七星螳螂拳白猿孝母

圖 26

12. 裏摟採三手
Brush inward and grab hand three times

（1）接上勢。兩腿步型不變；右拳變掌，向外、向上翻腕畫弧，隨即向裏摟手變拳，拳心向下，拳面向左，高與肩平；目視前方。（圖 26）

(1) Follow the above posture, keep the stance of the two legs changeless, change the right fist into palm, turn and swing the right wrist upward to draw a curve, then grab the right hand inward into fist, keep the fist – palm down and the fist –plane leftward, at shoulder hieght. Eyes look forward. (Figure 26)

圖 27

　　⑵上動不停。右拳收抱於腰間，拳心向上；同時，左掌向前摟抓變拳，拳心向下，高與肩平；目視前方。（圖 27）

　　⑵ Keep the above action, draw the right fist back and hold it on the waist with the fist–palm up. At the same time, grab the left palm forward into fist with the fist–palm down, at shoulder height. Eyes look forward.（Figure 27）

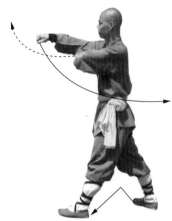

圖28

（3）上動不停。右拳自腰間向前沖拳，拳心向下，
拳面向前，高與肩平；同時，左拳屈臂回收於右肘
下，拳心向下，拳面向右；目視右拳。（圖28）

(3) Keep the above action, punch the right fist forward from
the waist, keep the fist–palm down and the fist–plane forward,
at shoulder height. At the same time, bend the left arm to draw
back the left fist under the right elbow, keep the fist–palm down
and the fist–plane outward. Eyes look at the right fist.（Figure
28）

（4）上動不停。右腳向左腳內側併步震腳；同時，
右拳向下、向後擺拳，拳心向後，置於右臀部；左拳
掄臂上擺，架於頭頂上方，拳心向下，拳眼向後；目

圖 29

視前方。（圖 29）

　　要點：採手迅速敏捷，沖拳力達拳面；震腳有力，挺胸收腹。

(4) Keep the above action, bring the right foot to gether to the inner side of the left one and stamp it. At the same time, swing the left fist downward and backward with the fist–palm backward, place it on the right buttock; swing the left arm upward, parry the left fist above the head, keep the fist–palm down and the fist– hole backward. Eyes look forward. (Figure 29)

　　Key points: picking the hand shall be quick and smart, the strength of punching the fist shall reach the fist–plane; stamping the foot shall be forceful, lift the chest and draw in the abdomen.

圖 30

13. 撩陰捶　crotch-uppercutting hammer

接上勢。左腳向前上一步，右腳隨即跟步，身體下蹲成蹬山步；同時，右拳從後向前、向上反撩，拳眼向裏，拳背斜向上，略低於肩；左拳變掌，從上向下迎擊右前臂；目視右拳。（圖30）

要點：上步迅速，右拳撩擊，力達拳背。

白猿孝母套路動作圖解

Follow the above posture, the left foot takes a step forward, then the right one follows up, the body squats into mountaineering step. At the same time, uppercut with the right fist from rear to upper front, keep the fist— hole inward and the fist—back up aslant, slightly lower than the shoulder; change the left fist into palm and counterpunch the right forearm upward to downward. Eyes look at the right fist. ﹝Figure 30﹞

Key points: stepping forward shall be quick, thrusting the right fist upward with the strength reaching the fist—back.

七
星
螳
螂
拳
白
猿
孝
母

圖 31

14. 左封右崩捶
Left wrap and right snap hammer

(1)接上勢。右腳向前上步，隨即左腳跟步，重心前移成蹬山步；同時，左手向前封抓變拳，拳心向下，高與肩平；右拳收抱於腰間，拳心向上；目視前方。（圖 31）

(1) Follow the above posture, the right foot steps forward, then the left one follows up, shift the barycenter forward into mountaineering step. At the same time, grab the left hand forward into fist, keep the fist–palm down at shoulder height; draw back the right fist and hold it on the waist with the fist–palm up. Eyes look forward. (Figure 31)

圖 32

(2)上動不停。左拳屈臂回收於右胸前，拳心向下，拳面向右；右拳經左前臂內側向前崩拳，拳心向裏，拳面向上，高與頜平；目視右拳。（圖 32）

要點：崩拳要有彈性，抖肩發力，力達拳背。

(2) Keep the above action, bend the left arm and draw the left fist to the front of the chest, keep the fist –palm down and the fist –plane outward; snap the right fist forward through the inner side of the left forearm, keep the fist–palm inward and the fist–plane up, at jaw height. Eyes look at the right fist. (Figure 32)

Key points: snap punch shall be flexible, snap the shoulders to send strength that shall reach the fist–back.

圖 33

15. 採三手玉環步
Grab hand three times in jade-ring step

（1）接上勢。身體起立，重心前移至右腿；同時，右手向外翻腕採抓變拳，拳心向下，拳面向前，高與肩平。（圖 33）

(1) Follow the above posture, the body stands up, move the barycenter to the right leg. At the same time, turn the right wrist outward and grab it into fist, keep the fist–palm down and the fist–plane forward, at shoulder height.（Figure 33）

圖 34

(2)上動不停。身體略微右轉成右弓步；同時，右拳收抱於腰間，拳心向上；左拳變掌，從胸前向前封抓變拳，拳心向下，拳面向右，高與肩平；目視左拳。（圖34）

(2) Keep the above action, slightly turn the body to the right into right bow stance. At the same time, draw the right fist back and hold it on the waist with the fist－palm up; change the left fist into palm, grab it forward through the front of the chest and change it into fist, keep the fist－palm down and the fist－plane of the rightward, at shoulder height. Eyes look at the left fist.（Figure 34）

七
星
螳
螂
拳
白
猿
孝
母

圖 35

　　(3)上動不停。身體略向左轉；同時，右拳經左前
臂內側向前上方沖出，拳心斜向上，高與鼻齊；左拳
回收於右胸前，拳心向下；目視右拳。（圖 35）

(3) Keep the above action, slightly turn the body to the left.
At the same time, punch the right fist upward ahead through the
inner side of the left forearm, keep the fist–palm up aslant at
nose level; draw back the left fist to the front of the chest with
the fist–palm down. Eyes look at the right fist.（Figure 35）

白
猿
孝
母
套
路
動
作
圖
解

圖 36

(4) 上動不停。身體向右轉 90°；右拳收抱於腰
間，拳心向上；左拳變掌，經右臂外側向前穿掌，掌
心斜向上，掌指向左前方；目視左掌。（圖 36）

(4) Keep the above action, twist and turn the body 90° to the
right, draw back the right fist and hold it on the waist with the
fist–palm up; change the left fist into palm and thread the palm
out forward through the outer side of the right arm, keep the
palm up aslant and the fingers leftward ahead. Eyes look at the
left palm. (Figure 36)

七星螳螂拳白猿孝母

圖 37

　　(5) 上動不停。左腳向前跨一步，隨即右腳跟步，身體向左轉 90°，蹲身成玉環步；同時，左掌翻腕變拳，向左側拉帶，拳心向外，拳眼向下，高與肩平；右拳變掌，經胸前向左下方推掌，置於左膝外側，掌心向左，掌指向前；目視左前方。（圖 37）

白
猿
孝
母
套
路
動
作
圖
解

(5) Keep the above action, the left foot strides a step forward, then the right one follows up, twist and turn the body leftward by 90° squats into jade-ring step. At the same time, turn the left wrist to change the left palm into fist and draw the fist to the left side, keep the fist-palm outward and the fist-hole down, at shoulder level; change the right fist into palm and horizontally push it left downward through the front of the chest, place it at the outer side of the left knee, keep the palm leftward and the fingers forward. Eyes look leftward ahead. (Figure 37)

圖 38

16. 左封右崩捶
Left wrap and right snap hammer

(1)接上勢。右腳向前跨一步，左腳隨即跟步，向下蹲身成蹬山步；同時，右掌變拳收抱於腰間，拳心向上；左手向裏封抓變拳，拳心向下，拳眼向裏，高與肩平；目視前方。（圖 38）

(1) Follow the above posture, the right foot strides a step forward, then the left foot follows up, squat into mountaineering step. At the same time, change the right palm into fist, draw the fist back and hold it on the waist with the fist–palm up; grab the left hand inward and change it into fist, keep the fist–palm down and the fist–hole inward, at shoulder height. Eyes look forward.
(Figure 38)

圖 39

(2)上動不停。左拳回收於右胸前，拳心向下，拳面向右；右拳經左前臂內側向前崩拳，拳心向裏，拳面向上，高與頜平；目視右拳。（圖 39）

要點：崩拳要有彈性，抖肩發力，力達拳背。

(2) Keep the above action, draw back the left fist to the front of the right chest, keep the fist–palm down and the fist–plane rightward; hurl the right fist forward through the inner side of the left forearm, keep the fist–palm inward and the fist–plane up, at jaw height. Eyes look at the right fist.〔Figure 39〕

Key points: snap punch shall be flexible, snap the shoulders to send strength that shall reach the fist–back.

圖 40

第三段 Section Three

17. 轉身掄劈圈捶
Turn body, swing, hack and circle hammer

(1)接上勢。身體起立，左轉 90°；同時，右拳內翻掄臂後擺，拳心向後，置於右臀後側；左臂隨身向上、向左掄擺，拳心向前，拳眼斜向上；目視左拳。（圖 40）

白
猿
孝
母
套
路
動
作
圖
解

(1) Follow the above posture, the body stands up and turns 90° to the left. At the same time, turn the right fist inward and swing the arm backward with the fist–palm backward, place it at the back of the right buttock; swing the left arm upward and leftward with body turn, keep the fist –palm forward and the fist–hole up aslant. Eyes look at the left fist. (Figure 40)

圖 41

(2)上動不停。身體左轉 90°，右腳跟抬起，重心前移至左腿；同時，左拳向下、向後掄擺，拳眼向下，高與肩平；右拳隨身向前、向下掄臂下劈，置於左膝前方，拳心向左，拳面斜向下；目視右拳。（圖 41）

(2) Keep the above action, turn the body 90° to the left, raise the right heel, shift the barycenter to the left leg. At the same time, swing the left fist downward and backward with the fist–hole down, at shoulder height: swing the right arm forward and downward with body turn and hack downward with the right fist, place it in front of the left knee, keep the fist–palm inward and the fist–plane down aslant. Eyes look at the right fist. (Figure 41)

圖 42

（3）上動不停。身體右轉 90°，右腳踏實，重心後移，左腿收回，腳尖點地成左虛步；同時，左拳由左向右圈擊，拳心向下，拳眼向裏；右拳變掌迎擊左前臂內側；目視左方。（圖 42）

要點：兩臂掄擺連貫迅速，圈捶力達拳面。

(3) Keep the above action, the body turns 90° to the right, the right foot lands firmly, shift the barycenter backward, draw the left leg back, with toes on ground into left empty stance. At the same time, circle –punch the left fist form leftward to rightward with the fist –palm down and the fist –hole inward; change the right fist into palm to counterpunch the inner side of the left forearm. Eyes look leftward.（Figure 42）

Key points: swinging the two arms shall be coherent and quick, the strength of circle punch shall reach the striking surface of the fist.

圖 43

18. 上步掄劈圈捶
Step forward, swing, hack and circle hammer

（1）接上勢。身體起立，左腳上半步踏實；左拳外翻向前劈砸，拳心向上，拳眼向右，高與腰齊；右掌變拳，向下、向後擺拳，拳心向下，高與肩平。（圖43）

(1) Follow the above posture, the body stands up, the left foot takes a half−step forward firmly. Turn the left fist outward and hack forward, keep the fist−palm up and the fist−hole right ward, at waist height; change the right palm into fist and swing it downward and backward with the fist−palm down, at shoulder height. (Figure 43)

圖44

（2）上動不停。右腳向左前方上一步，身體左轉
180°；同時，右拳從後向前掄劈，拳心向裏，拳輪向
下；左拳隨身向左、向上掄擺，拳心向下，拳眼向
左，高與肩平；目視右拳。（圖44）

(2) Keep the above action, the right foot takes a step left
forward, the body turns to the left by 180°. At the same time,
swing to hack with the right fist from backward to forward, keep
the fist–palm inward and the fist–wheel down; swing the left
fist leftward and upward with body turn, keep the fist–Palm
down and the fist–hole leftward, at shoulder height. Eyes look at
the right fist.（Figure 44）

圖 45

（3）上動不停。身體略向左轉；同時，右拳向前、向上掄擺，拳心向左，拳眼向上；左拳向後、向下掄擺，拳眼向下，兩臂呈一直線；目視右拳。（圖 45）

(3) Keep the above action, slightly twist and turn the body to the left. At the same time, swing the right fist forward and upward, keep the fist-palm leftward and the fist-hole up; swing the left fist backward and downward with the fist-hole down. The two arms shall be at the same heightl. Eyes look at the right fist.〔Figure 45〕

白
猿
孝
母
套
路
動
作
圖
解

圖 46

(4)上動不停。身體右轉 180°；同時，右拳隨身向
右、向後掄擺，拳眼向下，高與肩平；左拳向前、向
下掄劈，拳心向右，拳輪向下；目視左拳。（圖 46）

(4) Keep the above action, turn the body 180° to the right.
At the same time, swing the right fist rightward and backward
with body turn, keep the fist – hole down, at shoulder height;
swing and hack with the left fist forward and downward, keep
the fist – palm inward and the fist – wheel down. Eyes look at the
left fist.〔Figure 46〕

圖 47

（5）上動不停。身略左轉，重心後移至左腿，右腿提膝，腳尖內扣；同時，右拳從後向前、向左圈擊，拳面向裏，拳心向下，高與肩平；左拳變掌，從外向裏迎擊右前臂，掌心貼於右前臂內側；目視前方。（圖 47）

要點：整個動作連貫迅速，協調一致。

(5) Keep the above action, slightly turn the body to the left, shift the barycenter to the left leg, raise the right knee with toes inward. At the same time, circle punch the right fist backward to forward and leftward, keep the fist face inward and the fist – palm down, at shoulder height; change the left fist into palm and counterpunch the right forearm outward to inward, keep the palm close to the inner side of the right forearm. Eyes look forward. (Figure 47)

Key points: the whole action shall be coherent and quick, harmony and consistent.

圖 48

19.邦肘　Help elbow

接上勢。右腳向前落步，左腳隨即跟步，重心前移成蹬山步；同時，左掌變拳，兩拳交叉抱於胸前，左拳在裏，右拳在外，隨即左拳頂擊右腕向前平推，兩拳心均向下，目視前方。（圖 48）

要點：落步輕靈穩健，兩臂合力向前平推。

Follow the above posture, the right foot lands forward, then the left foot follows up, shift the barycenter forward into mountaineering step. At the same time, change the left palm into fist, cross the two fists and hold them in front of the chest, the left fist shall be inside while the right one outside, then the left fist strikes the right wrist and horizontally pushes forward. Both the palms shall be down. Eyes look forward. (Figure 48)

Key points: landing step shall be light and stable, the two arms horizontally push forward with resultand force.

圖 49

20. 左封右崩捶
Left wrap and right snap hammer

(1)接上勢。右腳向前上步，隨即左腳跟步，重心前移成蹬山步；同時，左手向前封抓變拳，拳心向下，高與肩平；右拳收於胸前，拳心向裏，拳面斜向上；目視前方。（圖 49）

(1)Follow the above posture, the right foot steps forward, then the left one follows up, shift the bary center forward into mountaineering step. At the same time, grab the left hand forward and change it into fist with the fist–palm down, at shoulder, height; draw back the right fist and hold it in front of the chest, keep the fist–palm inward and the fist–plane up aslant. Eyes look forward.（Figure 49）

圖 50

　　(2)上動不停。左拳屈臂回收於右胸前，拳心向
下，拳面向右；右拳經左前臂內側向前崩拳，拳心向
裏，拳面向上，高與頷平；目視右拳。（圖50）
　　要點：崩拳要有彈性，抖肩發力，力達拳背。

　　(2) Keep the above action, bend the left arm to draw back
the left fist and hold it in front of the right chest, keep the
fist–palm down and the fist–plane right ward; hurl the right fist
forward through the inner side of the left forearm, keep the
fist–palm inward and the fist–plane up, at chin height. Eyes look
at the right fist.（Figure 50）

　　Key points: snap punch shall be flexible, snap the shoulders
to send strength that shall reach the fist–back.

圖 51

21. 採三手玉環步
Garb hand three times in jade-ring step

（1）接上勢。身體起立，左腳跟抬起，重心前移至右腿；同時，右手向外翻腕採抓變拳，拳心向下，拳面向前，高與肩平。（圖 51）

(1) Follow the above posture, the body stands up, raise the left heel, move the barycenter forward to the right leg. At the same time, turn the right wrist outward and grab it into fist, keep the fist–palm down and the fist–plane forward, at shoulder height.（Figure 51）

圖 52

（2）上動不停。身體略微右轉；同時，右拳收抱於腰間，拳心向上；左拳變掌，從胸前向前封抓變拳，拳心向下，拳面向右，高與肩平；目視前方。（圖52）

（2）Keep the above action, slightly turn the body to the right. At the same time, draw, back the right fist and hold it on the waist with the fist-palm up; change the left fist into palm, grab it forward through the front of the chest, keep the fist-palm down and the fist-plane rightward, at shoulder level. Eyes look forward.（Figure 52）

白猿孝母套路動作圖解

圖 53

(3)上動不停。身體略向左轉；同時，右拳經左前臂內側向前上方沖出，拳心斜向上，高與鼻齊；左拳回收於右胸前，拳心向下；目視右拳。（圖 53）

(3) Keep the above action, slightly turn the body to the left. At the same time, punch the right fist forward ahead through the inner side of the left forearm, keep the fist–palm up aslant, at nose height; draw back the left fist and hold it in front of the chest with the fist–palm down. Eyes look at the right fost. (Figure 53)

圖 54

(4)上動不停。身體向右轉 90°；右拳收抱於腰間，拳心向上；左拳變掌，經右臂外側向前穿掌，掌心斜向上，掌指向左前方；目視左掌。（圖 54）

(4) Keep the above action, twist and turn the body 90° to the right, draw back the right fist and hold it on the waist with the fist–palm up; change the left fist into palm and thread the palm forward through the outer side of the right arm, keep the palm up aslant and the fingers left forward. Eyes look at the left palm. (Figure 54)

白猿孝母套路動作圖解

圖55

(5)上動不停。左腳向前跨一步，隨即右腳跟步，身體向左轉 90°，蹲身成玉環步；同時，左掌翻腕變拳，向左側拉帶，拳心向左，拳眼向下，高與肩平；右拳變掌，經胸前向左下方推掌，置於左膝外側，掌心向左，掌指向前；目視左前方。（圖55）

(5) Keep the above action, the left foot strides a step forward, then the right one follows up, twist and turn the body 90° to the left, squat into jade-ring step. At the same time, turn the left wrist and change the left palm into fist, draw it to the left side, keep the fist-palm left ward and the fist-hole down, at shoulder height; change the right fist into palm and horizontally push it left downward through the fornt of the chest, place it at the outer side of the left knee, keep the palm leftward and the fingers forward. Eyes look left forward. (Figure 55)

圖 56

第四段　Section Four

22. 鎖口捶　Mouth-locking hammer

（1）接上勢。身體起立，右轉 90°，抬右腳向前進步，左腳隨即跟步；同時，右掌變拳收於左腰前，掌心向上；左拳向下擺於左腰側，拳心向後，拳眼斜向下；目視右方。（圖 56）

(1) Follow the above posture, the body stands up and turns to 90° to the right, the right foot lifts and steps forward, then the left one follows up. At the same time, change the right palm into fist and draw it back to the front of the left waist with the fist-palm up; swing the left fist downward to the side of the left waist, keep the fist-palm backward and the fist-hole downward aslant. Eyes look rightward. (Figure 56)

圖 57

（2）上動不停。身體右轉 180°，左腳向前上一步，右腳跟步；同時，右臂屈肘，經胸前向右格肘，拳心向後，置於右耳側；左拳立拳向前平沖，拳心向右，高與肩平；目視左拳。（圖 57）

要點：上步，格肘與沖拳同時進行。

(2) Keep the above action, turn the body 180° to the right, the left foot takes a step forward, the right one follows up. At the same time, bend the right elbow through the front of the chest and parry the elbow rightward with the fist –palm backward, place it at the side of the right ear; horizontally punch the left fist forward with the thumb side up, keep the fist –palm rightward at shoulder height. Eyes look at the left fist.（Figure 57）

Key points: step forward, parrying the elbow and punching the fist shall be made simultaneously.

圖 58

23. 上步劈崩　Step forward to hack and snap

（1）接上勢。右腳向前上一步，重心前移成右弓步；右臂掄起，自後向前劈拳，拳心向左，拳輪向下，高與肩平；左拳變掌迎擊右前臂，掌指向上，掌心貼於右肘內側；目視右拳。（圖58）

(1) Follow the above posture, the right foot takes a step forward, shift the barycenter forward into right bow stance. Swing the right arm and hack the right fist backward to forward, keep the fist−palm leftward and the fist−palm down, at shoulder height; change the left fist into palm and counterpunch the right forearm, keep the fingers up ward and the palm close to the inner side of the right elbow. Eyes look at the right fist. (Figure 58)

圖 59

(2)上動不停。左掌向前封抓變拳，拳心向下，高
與肩平；右拳向下收於腹前，拳心向裏；目視前方。
（圖 59）

(2) Keep the above action, grab the left palm forward and
change it into fist with the fist－palm down, at shoulder height;
draw the right fist downward to the front of the abdomen with
the fist－palm inward. Eyes look forward.（Figure 59）

圖60

(3)上動不停。左拳屈臂回收於右胸前，拳心向下，拳面向右；右拳經左前臂內側向前崩拳，拳心向裏，拳面向上，高與頜平；目視右拳。（圖60）

要點：劈拳要以肩帶動掄臂下劈，力達拳輪，崩拳要擰腰抖肩，力達拳背。

白猿孝母套路動作圖解

(3) Keep the above action, bend the left arm and draw the left fist back to the front of the right chest, keep the fist–palm down and the fist–plane right ward; snap the right fist forward through the inner side of the left forearm, keep the fist –palm inward and the fist–plane of the fist up, at chin height. Eyes look at the right fist. (Figure 60)

Key points: hacking with the fist shall be driven by the shoulders and swinging the arm to hack downward, the strength shall reach the fit–wheel; snap punch shall be done by twisting the waist and snap the shoulders with the strength reaching the fist–back.

圖 61

24. 螳螂千眼 Mantis with thousand eyes

（1）接上勢。身體重心上提；右拳變掌，向下、向右畫掌於右胯側；左拳變掌向前經右臂外側畫出，掌心向前，掌指向右，高與肩平；目視左掌。（圖 61）

(1) Follow the above posture, raise the barycenter of the body. Change the right fist into palm and swing the palm downward and rightward to the side of the right hip; change the left fist into palm and swing it forward, keep the palm forward and the fingers rightward, through the outer side of the right arm at shoulder height. Eyes look at the left palm.（Figure 61）

圖 62

(2)上動不停。身體左轉 90°；同時，左掌向上、
向左畫掌，掌心向左置於左耳側；右掌隨身向上畫
弧，掌心向上，高與頭平；目視右掌。（圖 62）

(2) Keep the above action, turn the body 90° to the left. At
the same time, swing the left palm upward and leftward, place it
at the side of the left ear with the palm outward; swing the right
palm upward to draw a curve with body turn, keep the palm up,
at head height. Eyes look at the right palm.（Figure 62）

圖 63

（3）上動不停。身體下蹲成玉環步，上身向前傾斜；同時，左掌變鉤手，屈臂收於胸前，鉤尖向下；右掌向左經胸前變鉤手，再向右後方反撩，鉤尖向上，高與肩平；目視右後方。（圖 63）

(3) Keep the above action, squat into jade –ring step, slant the upper part of the body forward. At the same time, change the left palm into hook hand, bend the left arm to draw the hook hand to the front of the chest with the hook –tip downward; change the right palm into hook hand leftward through the front of the chest, then uppercut upward inversely to the right backward with the hook –tip upward, at shoulder height. Eyes look right backward.（Figure 63）

圖 64

25. 蓋陽掌玉環步
Cover with Yang-palm in jade-ring step

(1)接上勢。身體起立，右轉 180°，左腳跟提起，重心前移成叉步；同時，兩臂抱於胸前，左鈎手變掌置於右腋下，右鈎手變掌抱於左肘外側；目視左側。（圖 64）

(1) Follow the above posture, the body stands up and turns 180° to the right, raise the left heel, shift the barycenter forward into a cross step. At the same time, hold the two arms in front of the chest, change the left hook hand into palm and place it under the right armpit, change the right hook hand into palm and hold it at the outer side of the left elbow. Eyes look left side. (Figure 64)

七
星
螳
螂
拳
白
猿
孝
母

圖 65

　　(2)上動不停。右手變拳收於腰間，拳心向上；左掌從右臂外側向前蓋掌，掌心向上，掌指向前，高與頭頂平；目視左掌。（圖 65）

　　(2) Keep the above action, change the right hand into fist and hold it on the waist with the fist palm up, the left palm covers forward from the outer side of the right arm, keep the palm up and the fingers forward, at head top height.（Figure 65）

白猿孝母套路動作圖解

圖 66

　　(3)上動不停。左腳向前上一步，右腳隨即跟步，身體下蹲成玉環步；同時，左掌變拳，左臂屈肘向左拉帶，拳心向下，拳眼向右，高與肩平；右掌向左側平推掌，置於左膝外側，掌心向左，掌指向前；目視前方。（圖 66）

　　要點：上步快捷穩健，向左推掌要以腰胯帶動，與左臂勁力相合，協調一致。

(3) Keep the above action, the right foot takes a step forward, then the left one follows up, the body squats into jade – ring step. At the same time, change the left palm into fist, bend the left elbow and pull leftward, keep the fist – palm down and the fist – hole right ward, at shoulder height; horizontally push the right palm to the left side and place it at the outer side of the left knee, keep the palm leftward and the fingers forward. Eyes look forward.（Figure 66）

Key points: stepping forward shall be quick and stable, pushing the palm leftward shall be driven by the waist and crotch, the force shall coincide with that of the left arm, harmonious and consistent.

圖 67

26. 戳捶　Thrust hammer

(1)接上勢。身體起立，略向右轉；同時，左拳變掌向前探掌，掌心向右，掌指向前，高與肩平；右掌變拳收抱於腰間，拳心向上；目視前方。（圖 67）

(1) Follow the above posture, the body stands up and slightly turns to the right. At the same time, change the left fist into palm and stretch the palm forward, keep the palm rightward and the fingers forward, at shoulder height; change the right palm into fist and hold it on the waist with the fist－palm up. Eyes look forward. (Figure 67)

圖 68

（2）上動不停。右腳向前上步，左腳隨即跟步，重心前移成蹬山步；同時，右拳向前立拳平沖，拳心向左，高與肩平；左掌迎擊右拳面，掌指向上附於右肘內側；目視右拳。（圖 68）

(2) Keep the above action, the right foot steps forward, then the left one follows up, shift the barycenter forward into mountaineering stance. At the same time, horizontally punch the right standing fist forward, keep the fist –palm leftward at shoulder height; the leftpalm counterpunch the right fist –plane of the fist, keep the fingers upward and close to the inner side of the right elbow. Eyes look at the right fist.（Figure 68）

白猿孝母套路動作圖解

圖 69

27. 轉身雙封手
Turn body and close up two hands

（1）接上勢。身體起立，左轉身 180°，重心落於兩腿間；同時，右拳變掌，向右畫弧，兩掌交叉於腹前，掌心均向下；目視兩掌。（圖 69）

（1）Follow the above posture, the body stands up and turns 180° to the left, put the barycenter in the middle of the two legs. At the same time, change the right fist into palm and swing it rightward to draw a circle, cross the two palms in front of the abdomen with the palms down. Eyes look at the two palms. （Figure 69）

圖 70

(2)上動不停。身體略向後傾斜；同時，兩臂屈肘，兩掌在胸前翻轉絞手，右掌掌心向上，掌指向右，左掌心向右，兩掌高與頜平；目視前方。（圖70）

(2) Keep the above action, slant the body backward slightly. At the same time, bend the two elbows, turn over and twist the two palms in front of the chest, keep the right palm up, the fingers rightward, and the left palm rightward. The two palms shall be at chin height. Eyes look forward. (Figure 70)

圖 71

(3)上動不停。重心略前移；同時，右掌前探，掌心向前，虎口向上，高與肩平；左掌護於右肩前，掌指向上，掌心向右；目視右掌。（圖 71）

(3) Keep the above action, slightly move the barycenter forward. At the same time, stretch the right palm forward, keep the palm forward, tiger´s mouth up, at shoulder height; the left palm guards in front of the right shoulder, keep the fingers up and the palm right ward. Eyes look at the right palm. (Figure 71)

圖 72

(4)上動不停。右臂屈肘，右掌變為螳螂鉤，吊腕鉤拉於胸前，鉤尖向右；同時，左掌向前探，掌心向左，掌指向前，高與肩平；目視左掌。（圖72）

(4) Keep the above action, bend the right elbow, change the right palm into mantis hook, hang the wrist and draw it to the front of the chest with the hook-tip rightward. At the same time, stretch the left palm forward, keep the palm leftward and the fingers forward, at shoulder height. Eyes look at the left palm. (Figure 72)

圖 73

(5)上動不停。身體下蹲成玉環步；同時，左臂屈
肘，左鉤手吊腕回拉於左膝上方，略低於肩；目視左
前方。（圖 73）

(5) Keep the above action, squat the body, forming a jade-ring step. At the same time, bend the left elbow, hang the left hook hand and draw it back above the left knee, slightly lower than the shoulders. Eyes look left forward.（Figure 73）

圖 74

28. 收勢　Closing form

（1）身體重心提起，略向右轉身；同時，兩鉤手變掌，經胸前上托，隨即向兩側分掌，兩臂成水平，兩掌心向外，掌指向上；目視右掌。（圖 74）

（1）Lift the barycenter of the body and turn the body to the right slightly. At the same time, change two hook hands into palms to lift through the front of the chest, then separate the palms to both sides. Keep two arms horizontal, with the palms outward and the fingers up. Eyes look at the right palm.（Figure 74）

圖 75

　　(2)上動不停。左腳向右腳併步；同時，兩掌變拳
抱於腰間；目視前方。（圖 75）

　　(2) Keep the above action, bring the left foot and right one
together. At the same time, change two palms into fists and hold
on the waist. Eyes look forward.（Figure 75）

圖76

(3)上動不停。兩拳變掌，自然下垂於身體兩側；目視前方。（圖76）

要點：挺胸收腹，平心靜氣，體態自然，精神內斂。

(3) Keep the above action, change the fists into palms and drop at both sides of the body naturally. Eyes look forward. (Figure 76)

Key points: lift the chest, draw in the abdomen, posture is natural and vital energy collects inward.

全套動作示意圖
Demonstration of All the Action

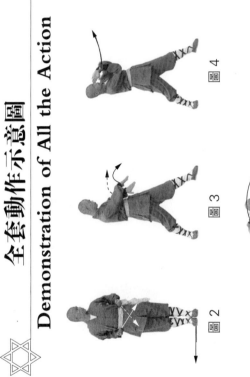

圖1　圖2　圖3　圖4　圖5
圖6　圖7　圖8　圖9　圖10

全套動作示意圖

七星螳螂拳白猿孝母

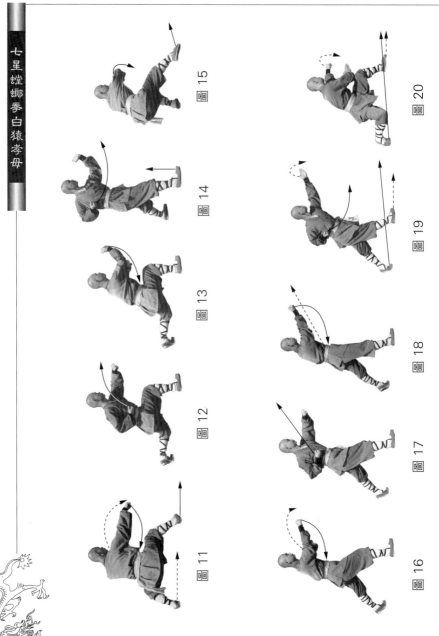

图 15

图 14

图 13

图 12

图 11

图 20

图 19

图 18

图 17

图 16

七星螳螂拳白猿孝母

圖 33

圖 32

圖 31

圖 30

圖 29

圖 38

圖 37

圖 36

圖 35

圖 34

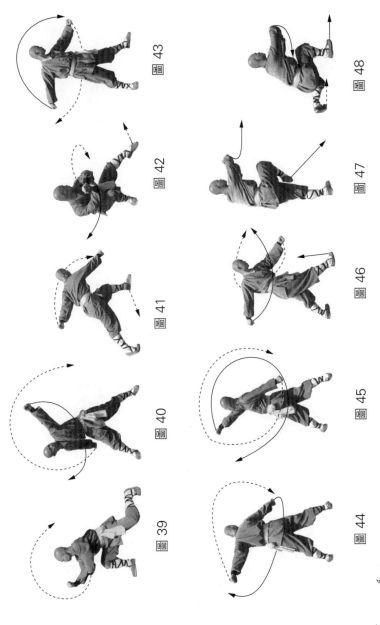

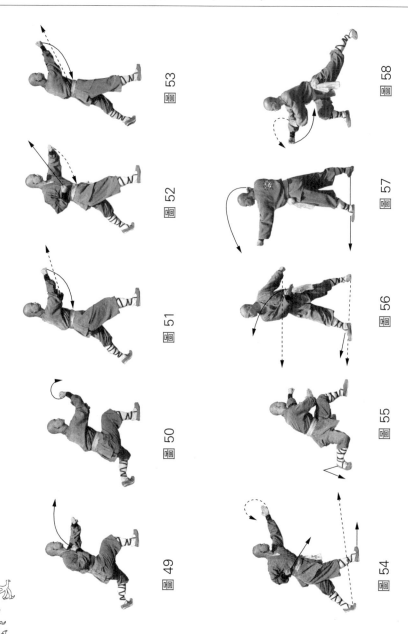

圖 53

圖 52

圖 51

圖 50

圖 49

圖 58

圖 57

圖 56

圖 55

圖 54

七星螳螂拳白猿孝母

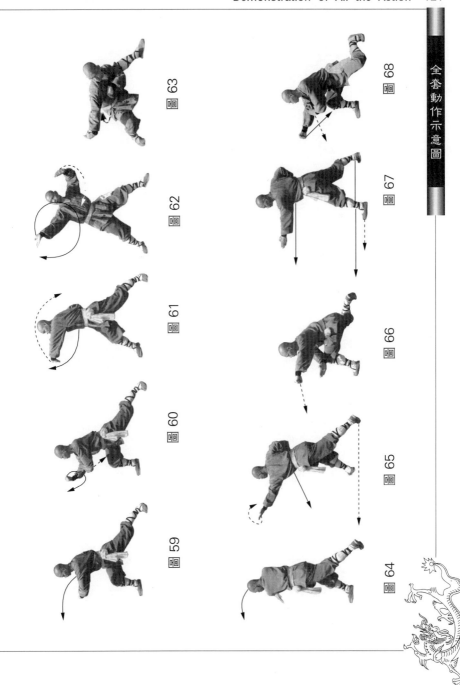

圖 63

圖 62

圖 61

圖 60

圖 59

圖 68

圖 67

圖 66

圖 65

圖 64

全套動作示意圖

七星螳螂拳白猿孝母

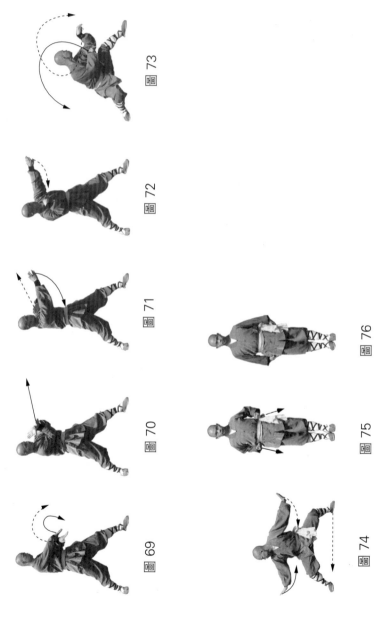

图 73

图 72

图 71

图 76

图 70

图 75

图 69

图 74

導引養生功 系列叢書

- ◎ 1. 疏筋壯骨功
- ◎ 2. 導引保健功
- ◎ 3. 頤身九段錦
- ◎ 4. 九九還童功
- ◎ 5. 舒心平血功
- ◎ 6. 益氣養肺功
- ◎ 7. 養生太極扇
- ◎ 8. 養生太極棒
- ◎ 9. 導引養生形體詩韻
- ◎ 10. 四十九式經絡動功

張廣德養生著作

每冊定價 350 元

全系列為彩色圖解附教學光碟

彩色圖解太極武術

1 太極功夫扇

定價220元

2 武當太極劍

定價220元

3 楊式太極劍

定價220元

4 楊式太極刀
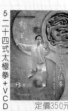
定價220元

5 二十四式太極拳+VCD

定價350元

6 三十二式太極劍+VCD

定價350元

7 四十二式太極劍+VCD

定價350元

8 四十二式太極拳+VCD

定價350元

9 楊式十八式太極劍

定價350元

10 楊氏二十八式太極拳+VCD

定價350元

11 楊式太極拳四十式+VCD

定價350元

12 陳式太極拳五十六式+VCD

定價350元

13 吳式太極拳五十六式+VCD

定價350元

14 精簡陳式太極拳八式十六式

定價220元

15 精簡吳式太極拳三十六式 拳架‧推手

定價220元

16 夕陽美功夫扇

定價220元

17 綜合四十八式太極拳+VCD

定價350元

18 三十二式太極拳 四段

定價220元

19 楊式三十七式太極拳+VCD

定價350元

20 楊氏五十一式太極劍+VCD

定價350元

古今養生保健法　強身健體增加身體免疫力

養生保健 系列叢書

中國氣功圖譜 *(無編號)* 定價250元	3 少林醫療氣功精粹 少林醫療氣功精粹 定價250元	4 龍形實用氣功 龍形實用氣功 定價220元

5 魚戲增視強身氣功 魚戲增視強身氣功 定價220元	7 道家玄牝氣功 道家玄牝氣功 定價200元	8 仙家秘傳袪病功 仙家秘傳袪病功 定價160元

少林十大健身功 少林十大健身功 定價180元	10 中國自控氣功 中國自控氣功 定價250元	11 醫療防癌氣功 醫療防癌氣功 定價250元

12 醫療強身氣功 醫療強身氣功 定價250元	13 醫療點穴氣功 醫療點穴氣功 定價250元	14 中國八卦如意功 中國八卦如意功 定價180元

三宗馬禮堂養氣功 定價420元	16 秘傳道家筋經內丹功 秘傳道家筋經內丹功 定價300元	17 三元開慧功 三元開慧功 定價250元

18 防癌治癌新氣功 防癌治癌新氣功 定價180元	19 禪定與佛家氣功修煉 禪定與佛家氣功修煉 定價200元	20 顛倒之術 顛倒之術 定價360元

簡明氣功辭典 定價360元	22 八卦三合功 八卦三合功 定價230元	23 朱砂掌健身養生功 朱砂掌健身養生功 定價250元

24 抗老功 抗老功 定價230元	25 意氣按穴排濁自療法 意氣按穴排濁自療法 定價250元	27 健身袪病小功法 健身袪病小功法 定價200元

張氏太極混元功 定價250元	29 中國璇密功 中國璇密功 定價250元	30 中國少林禪密功 中國少林禪密功 定價200元

31 郭林新氣功 郭林新氣功 定價400元	32 八卦之源與健身養生 太極 定價280元	33 現代原始氣功 現代原始氣功 定價400元

太極跤

1 太極防身術

定價300元

2 擒拿術

定價280元

3 中國式摔角

定價350元

簡化太極拳

1 陳式太極拳十三式

定價200元

2 楊式太極拳十三式

定價200元

3 吳式太極拳十三式

定價200元

4 武式太極拳十三式

定價200元

5 孫式太極拳十三式

定價200元

6 趙堡太極拳十三式

定價200元

原地太極拳

1 原地綜合太極二十四式

定價220元

2 原地活步太極四十二式

定價200元

3 原地簡化太極拳二十四式

定價200元

4 原地太極拳十二式

定價200元

5 原地青少年太極拳二十二式

定價220元

6 原地兒童太極拳十種16式

定價180元

健康加油站

1
糖尿病預防與治療

定價200元

2
胃部機能與強健

定價180元

3
不孕症治療

定價200元

4
簡易醫學急救法

定價200元

5
肥胖健康診療

定價200元

6
肝功能健康診療

定價200元

7
高血壓健康診療

定價200元

8
高血糖值健康診療

定價200元

9
尿酸值健康診療

定價200元

10
膽固醇中性脂肪健康診療

定價200元

11
痛風劇痛消除法

定價180元

12
三溫暖健康法

定價180元

13
手・腳病理按摩

定價180元

14
B型肝炎預防與治療

定價180元

15
吃得更漂亮、健康

定價180元

16
茶使您更健康

定價180元

17
圖解常見疾病運動療法

定價180元

18
科學健身改變亞健康

定價180元

國家圖書館出版品預行編目資料

七星螳螂拳白猿孝母／耿　軍　著
　　　——初版，——臺北市，大展，2006〔民95〕
　　　面；21公分，——（少林傳統功夫漢英對照系列；2）
　　　ISBN　978-957-468-510-3（平裝）

1.拳術—中國
528.97
95022967

七星螳螂拳白猿孝母

ISBN-13：978-957-468-510-3
ISBN-10：　　957-468-510-1

著　　者／耿　軍
責任編輯／孔　令　良
發 行 人／蔡　森　明
出 版 者／大展出版社有限公司
社　　址／台北市北投區（石牌）致遠一路2段12巷1號
電　　話／（02）28236031・28236033・28233123
傳　　眞／（02）28272069
郵政劃撥／01669551
網　　址／www.dah-jaan.com.tw
E - mail／service@dah-jaan.com.tw
登 記 證／局版臺業字第2171號
承 印 者／高星印刷品行
裝　　訂／建鑫印刷裝訂有限公司
排 版 者／弘益電腦排版有限公司
授 權 者／北京人民體育出版社
初版1刷／2007年（民96年）2月

定　價／180元

推理文學經典巨著，中文版正式授權

名偵探明智小五郎與怪盜的挑戰與鬥智
名偵探柯南、金田一都讚嘆不已

日本推理小說鼻祖－江戶川亂步

1894年10月21日出生於日本三重縣名張〈現在的名張市〉。本名平井太郎。
就讀於早稻田大學時就曾經閱讀許多英、美的推理小說。
畢業之後曾經任職於貿易公司，也曾經擔任舊書商、新聞記者等各種工作。
1923年4月，在『新青年』中發表「二錢銅幣」。
筆名江戶川亂步是根據推理小說的始祖艾德嘉‧亞藍波而取的。
後來致力於創作許多推理小說。
1936年配合「少年俱樂部」的要求所寫的『怪盜二十面相』極受人歡迎，
陸續發表『少年偵探團』、『妖怪博士』共26集……等
適合少年、少女閱讀的作品。

1 ～ 3 集 定價300元 試閱特價189元